"... absolutely compelling."
USA TODAY

"[R]efreshing and poignant..."
PUBLISHERS WEEKLY

"... just how a girl does it in this day and age."
ELLE MAGAZINE

"The book's charm lies in MariNaomi's amused and
loving perspective on her curious, tough, occasionally
foolish younger self: she knows she may have
misunderstood the dynamics of her relationships, but
she can still evoke the intensity of her feelings."
DOUGLAS WOLK,
THE NEW YORK TIMES

"[P]acked with wisdom and raw experience."
BUST MAGAZINE

"MariNaomi tells honest stories about her love
life. Sometimes they're sweet, sometimes painfully
embarrassing ... but they're so genuine every time."
BITCH MAGAZINE

Dragon's Breath and other true stories

comics by MariNaomi

Entire contents copyright © 2014 by MariNaomi

MariNaomi.com

Published by 2D Cloud and Uncivilized Books

Design by Justin Skarhus & Will Dinski

Production by Raighne Hogan

2D Cloud
P.O. Box 6281
Minneapolis, MN 55406
www.2dcloud.com

Uncivilized Books
P.O. Box 6534
Minneapolis, MN 55406
www.uncivilizedbooks.com

First Edition September 2014

10 9 8 7 6 5 4 3 2 1

Library of Congress Control Number: 2014937614

ISBN 978-1-941250-01-3

Distributed to the Trade by:
Consortium Book Sales & Distribution, LLC
34 Thirteenth Ave. NE, Suite 101
Minneapolis, MN 55413-1007
cbsd.com, Orders: (800) 283-3572

Printed in China

For Gary

Foreword

I haven't been what you'd call a serious reader of comics since my punk days in the '80s, and even then I wouldn't have thought of myself as an expert. I was passionate about *Love and Rockets* and *American Splendor*, kept up with *V for Vendetta* and a few other series. Pretty much just the big stuff. And then other things came along in my life to distract me—music, work, kids, food—so I'd been away from all this for many years the first time I encountered MariNaomi.

It was when her series debuted in *The Rumpus*, with a story called "Dragon's Breath," the title story of the book you are holding in your hand. I want you to go read it. Flip ahead and read it right now. Don't mind the bookstore lady, just act like you're shopping. It's cool, I'll wait here.

...doo doo, do deet doo, doo doo, do deet doo...

Did you see that? Wasn't it fantastic? (And that's only the first one. You've got a whole book's worth of that waiting for you.)

That story was the first time that Mari went right into my head, drilled straight into my brain and pushed one of my secret hidden buttons. And this particular button, which I'd been ignoring for years, filled me with panic. That story that Mari told, that story that you just read, that I first read on *The Rumpus* a couple of years ago, could have come straight from my life.

Her father is me. She is my kids. Her grandpa is my kids' grandpas, both my dad and my stepdad. The drinking, the smoking, the temper, the intolerance. The violence as a young father. And then the sweet old man who later in life loved his grandchild most of all.

5

I've never had that conversation with my kids. I've always wondered if I will have to someday, if it's even a good idea. So I asked Mari, right out there in *The Rumpus* comments where everyone can see:

"Mari, this is important to me. Do you wish you had never been told?"

And she answered me. She gave me a good, thoughtful, kind answer. It helped me.

And then I suppose every time she published another comic on *The Rumpus*, as her finger hovered over the Submit button, she wondered, "Good GOD, who am I going to have be a therapist for THIS time?"

#

Here's the thing that is special about MariNaomi. She notices people. And she sees things. The tiniest things. She has her eyes open all the time.

I met her at a comics convention in Austin once and we chatted for only about ten minutes while she signed my books. Then later that week in her online journal she knocked out a picture of me, totally from memory, that was so dead-on that when I showed it to my girlfriend, she squealed. "Eeeeeee!"

Just like that. Like a happy small animal. "Eeeeeee!"

My hair, my goatee, the way my tattoos peeked out a little from my sleeves, my reading glasses hanging from my collar, the way I held on to the pile of the too-many-books I bought with both hands while I tried to mansplain my way through something.

She has a great love for people and it shines out of every page of her work.

She sees the homeless guy outside the bank, and notices when he's not in his usual spot.

She sees the awkward guy at the copier place, and she feels loss when she understands the pain he lived with.

And she sees herself, her goodness and her selfishness, her joys and embarrassments, her lusts and her petty jealousies.

And somehow she manages to hold on to all of these things that she sees and hears, and keep them in her head long enough to get home and ink it all onto the page. Beautiful and deceptively simple in form, but complex in feeling. A detail here, an expression there.

An old woman in a sad housecoat, half hidden in a doorway. A lifetime's worth of regret and neglect.

A gun that is so heavy, yet so easy to shoot.

A man in a crime report, who terrorized a neighborhood but once was a pretty brown-eyed baby.

There's one more piece in here, which you can flip ahead and read now if you want to, if Mari will indulge me, or I could just describe it to you, because it sums up in three simple pages everything that you need to know. It's called "Independence Day." Go find it.

It's about a teenage runaway Mari, learning to be scrappy, hanging out on a dark beach with some "new friends." Walking in the sand, smoking, trying to be tough.

Then, something happens. Something bright and glowing and magical.

This is MariNaomi land. Something magical always happens. If you keep your eyes open.

Keep walking, and keep looking.

Step.

I've heard of this happening!

Step.

Let the rest of the world fade away into white noise. Just keep reading. Keep looking.

Step.

Step.

Step.

Step...

—Ray Shea, Austin, TX

TABLE of CONTENTS

The stories in this book first appeared in
Smoke In Your Eyes on theRumpus.net, with
the following exceptions:

"He Sees You When You're Sleeping" (page 49)
and "For the Greater Good" (page 327)
first appeared in Frisco al Fresco on SFBay.CA.

"The Rebound" (page 171) first appeared in
This Isn't Working: Comics About Ex-boyfriends
(Paper Rocket Minicomics).

"In Case of Emergency" (page 291) first
appeared in *Transit Comics and Stories.*

DRAGON'S BREATH

MY GRANDPA WAS DIAGNOSED WITH CIRRHOSIS OF THE LIVER WHEN HE WAS FIFTY-FIVE YEARS OLD.

HE LASTED ANOTHER TWENTY YEARS, A TUMBLER OF WHISKEY IN HIS HAND 'TIL THE END.

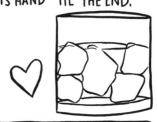

MANY YEARS AFTER HE PASSED AWAY...

APPARENTLY HIS ALCOHOLISM HAD A DARK SIDE. (fig. 1-3)

16

DOWN THE RABBIT HOLE

1979, MIDDLE OF NOWHERE, TEXAS PANHANDLE

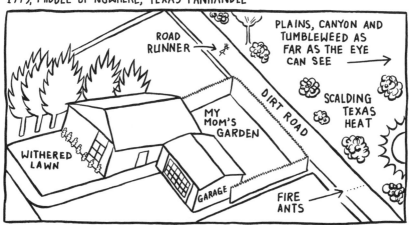

MY MOM WAS NOT FOND OF VISITORS IN HER VEGETABLE GARDEN.

THE MAMA RABBIT DIDN'T RETURN.

WE KEPT THEM SOMEPLACE NICE AND COOL.

ONE DAY...   ...AND THE NEXT DAY...

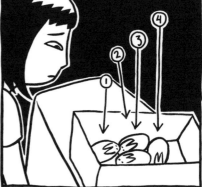

21

MY MOM CALLED A NEIGHBOR, WHO SAID HE'D BE RIGHT OVER.

ALL THE CRYING IN THE WORLD WASN'T GOING TO SAVE THAT SNAKE'S LIFE.

LEAVING HOME

ONCE UPON A TIME, I WAS AN OBEDIENT CHILD.

BUT IN MY RECURRING DREAM, THE FACT THAT

I WASN'T ALLOWED
IN THE DESERT
      WILDERNESS
BEHIND OUR HOUSE
        DIDN'T
          MATTER.

I FOLLOWED THE SAME PATH NIGHTLY, AND
      GOT A LITTLE BIT CLOSER EACH TIME.

FINALLY ONE NIGHT, I APPROACHED MY DESTINATION.

WE WERE MOVING SOON, SO MY PARENTS LET
ME HAVE A GOOD-BYE SLUMBER PARTY.

It's getting HOT.

I WASN'T THE ONLY ONE
    WHO DIDN'T MAKE IT TO THE CAVE.

ONLY ONE OF US GOT THERE.

THAT NIGHT, IN MY DREAM, I ENTERED THE CAVE.

AFTER WE MOVED, I NEVER WENT BACK.

MARINAOMI 2012

UNREASONABLE DEMANDS, PART 1

43

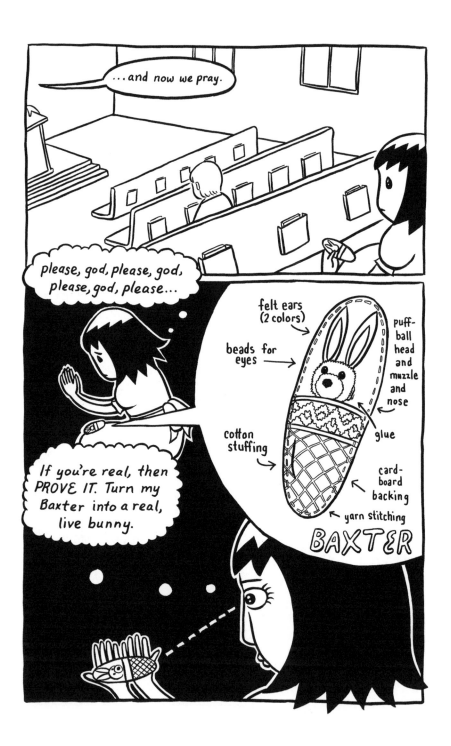

44

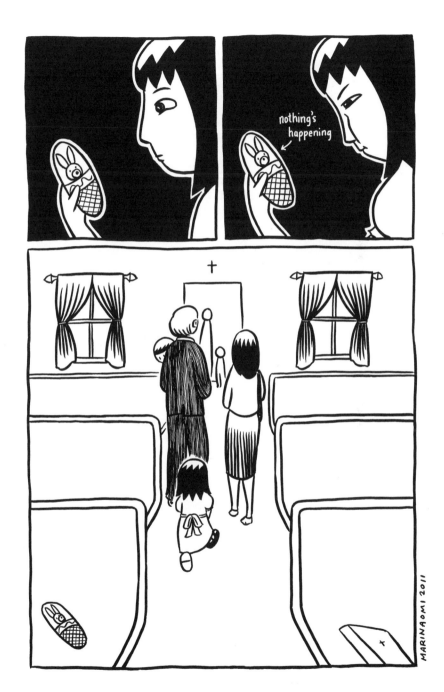

47

HE SEES YOU WHEN YOU'RE SLEEPING

~ SHUFFLE SHUFFLE ~

They'd better go to
bed or Santa's never
going to get here.

MARINAOMI 2012

THE QUITS

I ATTEMPTED QUITTING MANY TIMES OVER THE YEARS, BUT IT WASN'T UNTIL I WAS THIRTY THAT I MANAGED TO KICK THE HABIT FOR GOOD.

Rest in peace, Aunt Mary.

MR. VANONI

MR. VANONI WAS MY HIGH SCHOOL BIOLOGY TEACHER.

HIS TEACHING STYLE WAS DRY AND TEXTBOOK-DRIVEN.

BUT EVERY ONCE IN A WHILE, DURING A LECTURE...

HE'D TAKE OUT HENRY...

FLIP HIM OVER, AND RUB HIS BELLY UNTIL HE DRIFTED OFF TO SLEEP.

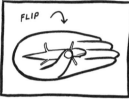

EACH TIME, I WAS JUST AS MESMERIZED AS THE LIZARD.

AFTER I DROPPED OUT OF SCHOOL, A TEACHER DIED OF AIDS.

"CHUCK" SMITH
SOCIAL STUDIES GURU
PASSIONATE
CHARISMATIC
OWNED COUNTLESS
PINK SWEATER VESTS

AN ENTIRE SECTION OF THE YEARBOOK WAS DEDICATED TO HIM.

We love you, Mr. Smith!

ONLY A MONTH OR SO LATER, MR. VANONI DIED UNEXPECTEDLY.

HIS YEARBOOK MEMORIAL WAS TINY BY COMPARISON.

I'm sure they just ran out of space.

Mr. V →

←Mr. S

REST IN PEACE, MR. VANONI.

PET

PET

INDEPENDENCE DAY

INDEPENDENCE DAY 1988

I'd been a runaway for about a month, and I was getting used to being on my own, becoming scrappy.

I was less afraid of the present but more nervous about what the future might hold.

Some new friends and I hitched a ride to the beach.

It was so dark that when I lit my cigarette, the flame lived on in my corneas long after it had gone out.

When I stepped onto the sand,
something magical happened.

MARINAOMI 2012

GONE

I've been thinking about my ex-boyfriend, Jason, wondering what became of him. Maybe it's true that he died in an awful car accident,

or maybe that's just a rumor

but I find it hard to believe that he just isn't anywhere at all. Sometimes when he appears in my dreams, I can't help but feel like he's haunting me. But I know it's naïve of me to assume he'd even remember my name.

I was sixteen and in love for the first time, he was twenty-one, with lots of experience in life and love. There was a lot going on at the time, too—he was trying to launch a new career, plus four out of the six months of our relationship were spent with him in jail.

And those other two months weren't so great, if you look at it from a distance. He cheated on me, he was grumpy and he was always kind of hustling, vying for his next quick buck. BUT he was also beautiful. He scrutinized the world through passionate lenses, he always pulled himself up. He examined his faults, and he desperately wanted to be a better person. I've never seen such a genuine attempt at self-improvement.

I'm going to be an international model.

I've never admitted to cheating on someone before. And I've cheated on everybody.

He felt awful for the hurt he'd inflicted on people he cared about. He wanted to make amends.

75

He was reforming, and then he went to jail. All those self-help books he asked me to send him, all those hours spent in AA, even though he wasn't a drinker...All those letters he wrote me from jail—I saved each and every one—telling me how hard it was to stay "good" while surrounded by the criminally minded.

But I'm trying

I'm trying!

I can feel myself slipping into my old mindset

I remember this one night when he was living in a house in Fairfax with a dozen other guys and a coke dealer who was on the lease. Jason and this guy Chris lived in tents in the basement.

Sweet, soft-spoken Chris who later freaked out at a supermarket on LSD, went to prison, then spent the rest of his short life as a homeless schizophrenic before throwing himself under a BART train.

REST IN PEACE

That night, Jason had just admitted something to me—I don't remember if it was about the cheating or if it was some other dark secret—and I was in shock. We had run out of words for each other and were going to sleep on it, but when he opened the door, the whole world changed.

For one thing, the wall in front of us toppled before our eyes.

We stood there, slack-jawed, and once the dust cleared, saw two of his roommates in the next room.

I never figured out if they planned it that way, if they knew someone was coming home at that moment and had synchronized the demolition of that wall to the opening of the door. How could they? Regardless, the timing was impeccable.

The boys were having an eviction party because the coke dealer had stolen everyone's rent money and they were all getting kicked out, all those lost young men with no place to go, no family, no money. The walls were spray painted then hammered into pulp. All the coke dealer's worldly possessions were destroyed—his recording equipment, his car, his keyboards. Never fuck over people who've got nothing to lose. I mean it.

PETER THE COKE DEALER

77

I remember following this one skinhead around, using my own can of spray paint to correct his spelling errors. Even as a sixteen-year-old high school dropout I was meticulous about spelling. But come on, how can you misspell expletives? It's embarrassing.

Jason and I were already so drained when we walked through that door, and it didn't take long before the same question presented itself on everyone's brow.

FSSSSSSSSSSSSHH!

RED

I call DIBS on sleepin' in PETE'S CAR.

Didn't you throw his TV through its windshield?

Yeah, that's how I'm gettin' into the back.

(Damn.)

Jason gathered his things and loaded up his VW bus.

We drove out to China Beach and parked by the side of the road and passed out, the bad stuff behind us, left in the rubble.

MAKESHIFT CURTAINS TO KEEP OUT SUNLIGHT AND COPS' FLASHLIGHTS

SPOONING UNDER STINKY SHEETS ♡

The next morning we watched the sun rise with a Violent Femmes album in the tape deck. I screamed along to lyrics I didn't know yet. It's one of my happiest memories, even though it happened a million years ago.

I can't say I've regretted my decision not to be with Jason after he got out of jail, despite so many years of missing him. I was young, but I was old enough to recognize that there'd been too much drama between us in so short a time. I couldn't let his felony conviction hold me back. I was only

sixteen. I wanted to see the world. He ended up traveling the world long before me — I didn't really start until I was in my late twenties, which is a much different experience than it would've been as a teenager. For one thing, I'm safer as an adult. I have places to stay, money to pad me, should anything go horribly wrong. I'm also lonelier than I probably would've been, back when I was fearless and could talk to anyone. I'm more reserved now, less inclined to pry the life story out of a stranger, something I used to do all the time. It was one of the things that Jason used to love about me and now it's GONE.

But even though I'm a different person now, I know we could still appreciate each other, no matter what we've both become. It's this reason that I've searched for him through old phone numbers, mutual friends and the internet.

YAHOO! friendster myspace facebook Google

I even spent money on one of those internet searches, got his last dozen known addresses, hoping I was writing to the right person. I hand wrote a dozen letters and sent them into the world.

Jason? Is this you?

Please write back

Be my friend again

I'm sorry I cut you loose

Most
of the letters got returned to sender.
Some of them didn't. One got written on
and sent back, an anonymous rage of a note
warning me of Jason's wicked ways.

A WORD OF ADVICE: STAY AWAY FROM THAT BUM. HE USES PEOPLE! HE IS A BAD MAN. HE'LL TAKE ADVANTAGE OF YOUR GOODWILL!

When I saw that angry scrawl, two
pages of raw hurt, my heart sank. All
that time he spent trying to make himself a better person... How can all that be GONE?

MAKINAOMI 2012

WHEN YOU'RE YOUNG

I got my first leather jacket when I was sixteen.

It was sort of a gift from a guy I worked with at a fancy restaurant in Mill Valley.

He was a waiter and I was the clumsiest busser in the history of restaurants.

girlfriend, please!

↑
Did people talk like this yet in 1989?

H A N D S O M E

SCOTT
(I can't remember his last name)

After our shifts he'd drive us to the waterfront. We smoked and watched the sky get lighter.

what's your boyfriend in jail for anyway?

He's not my boyfriend.

Not any more.

When Scott made me laugh, it didn't matter that I was a high school dropout still living with my parents, working in a dead-end job.

He was the only friend of mine not trying to get into my pants.

I was so lonely.

When you're young, everything is meaningful.

Months later, I decided to quit my job before they could fire me.

Here, before I forget, your tips for tonight...

When we drove to our spot, Scotty started to cry.

Scotty, this is too much!

I know. Get yourself that leather jacket you liked on Haight St.

And don't ever forget me, okay?

Don't be stupid! Why would I forget you?

I carried that jacket around for
the next two decades.

I wish I could remember
his last name.

Masto 2012

KICK-ASS BOOTS

93

BUT JO, SHE WAS *really* BAD-ASS.

IT WASN'T LONG BEFORE SHAWNA WAS TAKING HER
HUMILIATION OUT ON THE WEAK.

I KEPT AN EYE OUT FOR HER, ALWAYS WAITING FOR
THAT MOMENT. I WASN'T AFRAID. I WAS CONFIDENT
THAT SHAWNA'D RUN AWAY CRYING AGAIN.

IT TOOK A LONG TIME FOR ME TO RUN INTO HER.
BY THIS TIME I WORKED AT A BANK AND ONLY
WORE MY BOOTS ON WEEKENDS.

SOMETHING WAS DIFFERENT ABOUT HER.

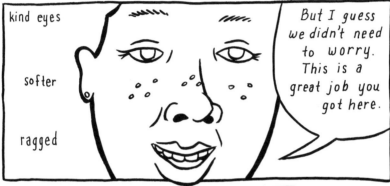

kind eyes

softer

ragged

But I guess we didn't need to worry. This is a great job you got here.

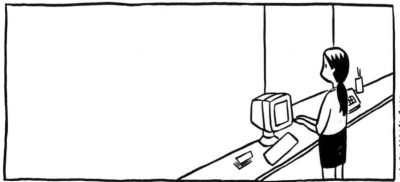

SONG IN MY HEAD

WHEN I WAS SEVENTEEN, I WAS SPORADICALLY
EMPLOYED, OUT OF SCHOOL, AIMLESS...

JEROME WAS MY SECOND-FAVORITE MILL VALLEY DENIZEN TO SHOOT THE SHIT WITH.

HE WAS PRETTY NUTS, BUT HE WASN'T THAT WEIRD COMPARED TO THE REST OF THE TOWN.

TWO YEARS LATER, I HAD A STEADY JOB
IN DOWNTOWN MILL VALLEY.

conformist on the outside →

← but not on the inside

ONE DAY, JEROME SAT OUTSIDE SINGING THE
SAME LINE FROM A SONG, OVER AND OVER AGAIN.

WHOA-OA HERE SHE COMES

WHOA-OA HERE SHE COMES*

* from "Maneater"
by Hall & Oates

AT FIRST I ASSUMED HIS INTENTION WAS
TO PISS OFF SOME YUPPIES.

BUT AS THE HOURS WENT BY, THE REALITY OF HIS
MENTAL CONDITION SANK IN.

EVER SINCE THEN, EACH TIME I GET A SONG
STUCK IN MY HEAD, I'M REMINDED OF JEROME.

*If I can't get it out of my head,
will this song drive me crazy?*

MARINAOMI 2013

108

INNER BEAUTY

BART train suicide was Mill Valley man

SAN FRANCISCO The man who killed himself by jumping in front of a BART train at the Civic Center BART station Thursday morning has been identified as Christopher ▬▬▬▬▬ of Mill Valley.

Described by Mill Valley Police as a "street person," ▬▬▬, 25, had been living on and off in the Marin County community since 1988.

At 5:30 p.m. Wednesday, ▬▬▬ called Mill Valley Police and said he wanted to go to a crisis center. But while talking to an officer, "he seemed to stabilize and declined to go to the center," according to the San Francisco Medical Examiner's report.

Shortly before 8 a.m. Thursday, ▬▬▬ jumped in front of a 10-car Richmond-bound BART train.

WHAT'S NEW, PUSSYCAT?

One time, I rode all the way to Custer's Last Stand to save him.

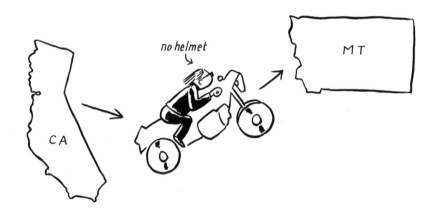

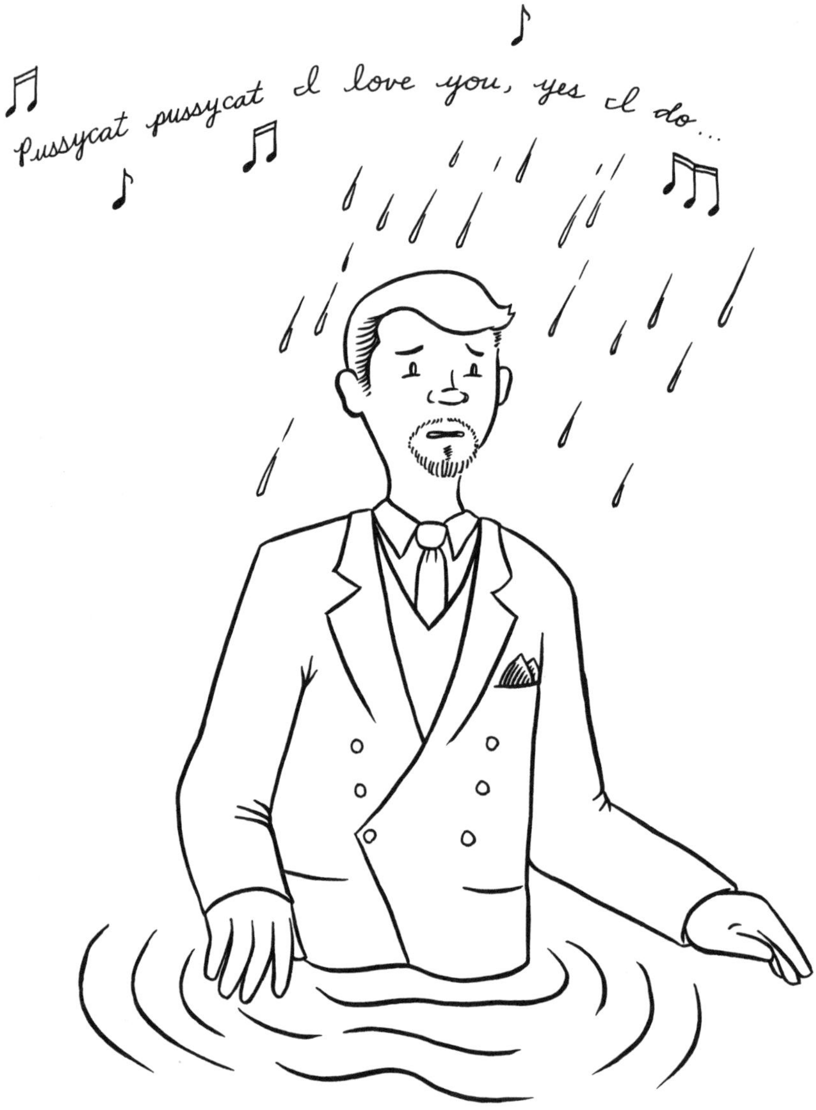
Pussycat pussycat I love you, yes I do...

MARINAOMI 2013

163

THE WRITER

THE WRITER

LATE 1990's ~ NOB HILL, SAN FRANCISCO, CALIFORNIA

I love it! It's in the middle of the city but it's so quiet!

Have you had a lot of applicants?

Naw, it just went on the market. If you got good credit, it's yours.

Oh wow, is that courtyard painted blue and green to look like a park?!

Sweet!

Yeh, but the tree is real.

There's just one thing...

The downstairs neighbor is a pain in the ass.

He always complains about the noise.

I just ignore him.

I'D ALWAYS PRIDED MYSELF ON BEING A GOOD NEIGHBOR,

LEVEL-HEADED,

THE KIND OF PERSON WHO COULD DIFFUSE A DIFFICULT SITUATION.

Don't worry.

I'm pretty sure I can handle him.

THE REBOUND

THE REBOUND

A TRUE TALE, WITH NAMES CHANGED, BY MARINAOMI ♡

JOE WAS A COWORKER I MET OVER EMAIL. WE BECAME FAST FRIENDS, CHATTING ELECTRONICALLY BACK AND FORTH ON COMPANY TIME.

IT WAS STRANGE MEETING HIM IN PERSON. HE WASN'T WHAT I HAD EXPECTED.

Konnichiwa, Mari-chan.

Bow

Did he really just speak Japanese to me? Eeew!

NOTE: WHITE GUYS WHO TRY TO CONNECT WITH MY ASIAN SIDE CREEP ME THE FUCK OUT.

I WAS IN THE HR DEPARTMENT, SO I HAD AN INFORMATIONAL ADVANTAGE.

He lived with his girlfriend last year, so he can't be a total loser, can he?

Age: 26

Ex-girlfriend prev. on health plan as domestic partner

Salary: Privileged

WE PLANNED TO MEET FOR LUNCH ON THE PREMISE THAT HE'D TEACH ME HOW TO USE PHOTOSHOP.

MY FIANCÉE

You never wear jewelry for ME.

I DIDN'T LEARN PHOTOSHOP THAT DAY.

This is really hard!

Shall we take a break?

I WAS GOING THROUGH A HARD TIME WITH MY FIANCÉE. IT WAS GOOD TO HAVE SOMEONE TO TALK TO.

When we started going out, he told me he didn't need to have kids, but now I'm starting to think he was just telling me what I wanted to hear.

That's dishonest.

173

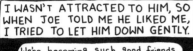
I WASN'T ATTRACTED TO HIM, SO WHEN JOE TOLD ME HE LIKED ME, I TRIED TO LET HIM DOWN GENTLY.

We're becoming such good friends. Why complicate it with sex? Besides, I'm engaged to Giuseppe and I want to make that work.

But...

THE DAY AFTER A MAJOR FIGHT WITH GIUSEPPE, JOE SENT ME THIRTEEN DOZEN LONG-STEMMED RED ROSES AT WORK.

Aargh!

Poop.

AFTER GIUSEPPE MOVED OUT, JOE WENT INTO OVERDRIVE. IT WAS IRRITATING, BUT ALSO FLATTERING, HIS PERSISTENCE.

I really just want to be alone right now. But maybe someday, when I'm in a better place...

But what if it's too late then, and I'm with someone else?! You don't want to let something this good slip away. Trust me!

EVENTUALLY, HE WORE ME DOWN.

Aw, what the hell. You only live once.

I'LL ADMIT IT WAS NICE TO FEEL WANTED.

HE TAUGHT ME TECHNIQUES HE LEARNED IN ART SCHOOL. I SHARED THINGS I'D FIGURED OUT ON MY OWN.

Mari, I admire you so much. Your work is so inspiring.

SKETCHING ← WITH PASTELS ↓

I WAS HEADY WITH HIS FLATTERY.

WE WERE LIBERALLY USING THE L-WORD BY THE TIME I DISCOVERED HE'D BEEN PURSUING ANOTHER COWORKER AT THE SAME TIME AS ME. SOMEHOW HE CONVINCED ME NOT TO LEAVE, BUT EVERYTHING CHANGED AT THAT MOMENT.

So... I was just the fish that bit first?

I BECAME JEALOUS AND PARANOID. I ASKED HIM ABOUT EVERY PRETTY GIRL WE SAW, THEN FELT INADEQUATE WHEN HE'D ADMIT HIS ATTRACTION.

WHEN I TOLD HIM MY EXES HAD BEEN SIMILAR TO ME IN THEIR PSYCHIC MONOGAMY, HE QUESTIONED THEIR HONESTY, AND SO, THUS, DID I.

I BEGAN TO DOUBT EVERYONE I'D EVER LOVED BEFORE HIM. I BEGAN TO DOUBT MYSELF.

HIS JEALOUSY WAS LIMITLESS. WHEN MY SISTER GOT MARRIED, JOE MOPED THE ENTIRE WEDDING.

Hold on, sis...

ok!

What has gotten INTO you?

You could be paying ME more attention, you know!

ONE DAY...

Why do you still hold onto all this D&D stuff?

I'd like to give it to our kids one day.

THIS WAS THE STRAW THAT BROKE THE CAMEL'S BACK.

KIDS?! But you KNOW I don't want kids!!!

Oh relax! I'm sure you'll change your mind.*

Besides, I don't need to start for another year or two.

*NOPE! I NEVER DID!

I WISH I COULD SAY THAT THIS EXPERIENCE TAUGHT ME A VALUABLE LESSON — THAT REBOUNDS CAN BE EVEN MESSIER THAN THE BREAKUPS THEY'RE MEANT TO PAD — BUT I WASN'T QUITE THERE YET.

Aw, what the hell. You only live once.

THIS ONE'S GONNA BE EVEN MESSIER, FOLKS!

making out in a bar (CLASSY!)

MARINAOMI 2010

177

UNREASONABLE DEMANDS, PART 2

182

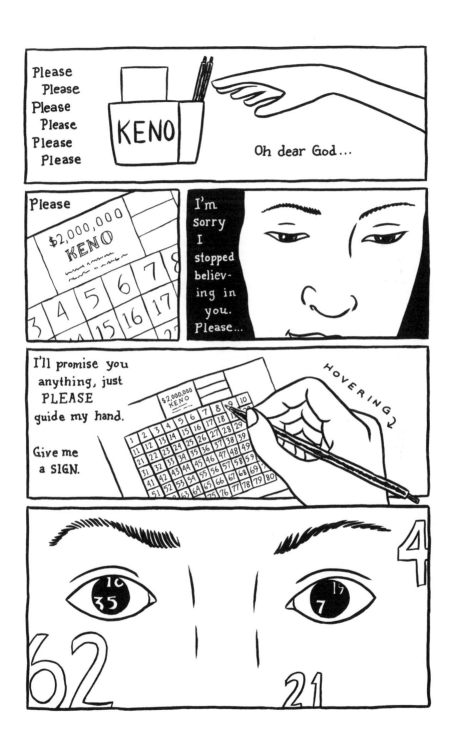

187

A DAY AT THE SHOOTING RANGE

2002

IT'S SO HEAVY.

THIS IS KIND OF FUN.

Wow, you're good!

Well I've played a lot of video games...

IT'S SO WEIRD THAT THESE
THINGS KILL PEOPLE.

Okay, my turn.

EASY-PEASY.

OH
FUCK.

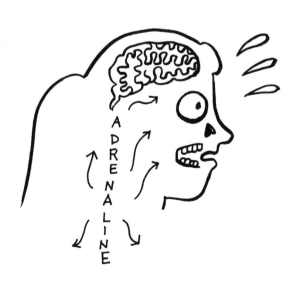

IT WOULD BE SO EASY.

IT WAS SO HEAVY.

MARINAOMI 2012

SLEEP DEPRIVED

I was so tired.

I hadn't slept in ages.

My eyes were sagging, my nerves shot, and my arms were covered in welts.

How did this happen, you may wonder?

Sit back, my friend, and let me tell you this chilling tale.

It all started with a consoling hang-out session with my old friend Cam, who was going through a hard time.

Cam was in the process of separating from his wife. He was holed up in a tiny, ramshackle studio in San Francisco's Tenderloin district, subletted from a sensual masseuse named Ilsa he'd found on Craig's List.

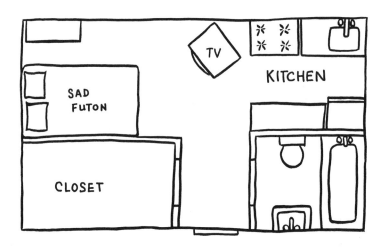

All her stuff lived there, her massage oil-scented life crammed into the walk-in closet whose door Cam never opened.

I examined the inflamed red bumps on his arm and suggested it might be stress-related. Still, I made sure not to brush arms with him, just in case.

Weeks, maybe a month later, we had just consummated the end of our just-friends-ship, upgraded to include benefits. As I drifted off to sleep on his sad bachelor's futon, a feeling of itchiness overcame me.

I assumed it was an allergic reaction to the detergent he washed his sheets with.

"I've got to go," I said, and tried to assure him I wasn't being squirrelly. This wasn't me being relationship-phobic (although it's true, I was), I just couldn't stand the itch.

"Call me?" Cam asked, and I agreed that I would.

I began the trek
up to my apartment
in Nob Hill,
wondering if I
should've slept
with my friend,
and thinking
probably not.

Days later, the itch was still
there. I had scratched so
much that there were giant
welts forming on my arms
and legs.

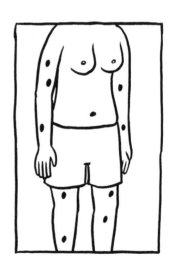

I haven't been able to sleep.

I miss you, too.

No, that's not what I meant! And please stop talking to me like I'm your girlfriend.

I'm sorry. I don't want to scare you off. Because I know that we're meant to be together.

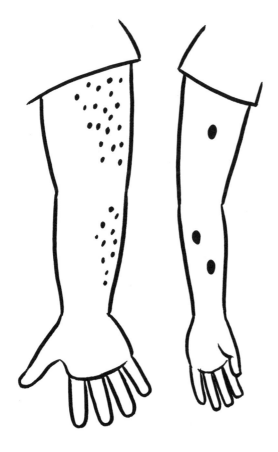

We compared rashes. Mine looked pretty different from his, but it seemed like too much of a coincidence.

Cam had gone to a number of dermatologists, but no one seemed to know what was going on.

The last doctor suggested it might be scabies and took a biopsy.

Terrified of what insecticide might do to my sensitive skin, I scheduled a dermatologist appointment for myself.

"Let me know what they say," Cam said, sounding a little scared.

"Bites," said the youthful Chinese doctor.
"You're getting bitten by something."

"Are you sure it isn't scabies?" I asked.

"Quite sure," he said,
noting that my
belly button was
clear and free of
bites, and that the
navel is a mite's
favorite place to roost.

He prescribed some cream and recommended
Claritin, and I went on my way.

As I exited the building, I phoned Cam to report the prognosis. But before I could get into it, he said, "I found a bug. Under the futon."

He described a strange kind of insect, a tick-like creature that moved too slow to save itself.

When he squished it, the bug exploded with what was clearly his blood. This sounded eerily like stories I'd heard as a child.

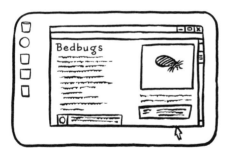

A bit of internet research came up with photos of bedbugs, which I emailed him.

"What do you think?" I asked. "Is this the culprit?"

"I dunno," he said. "The color was different."

That day, Cam received a
visit from the exterminator,
a tall guy named Jeffrey.

Sure enough, bedbugs
abounded.

"When he opened up the door to the
walk-in closet," Cam told me, "at first
I thought the wall was painted black."

"But then I
realized it
was
moving!"

An entire colony infested
Ilsa's dresser, and clearly it
had been there for awhile;
generations of bugs had
bored holes into it.

A large bug ambled by, and the exterminator popped it dead with his flashlight.

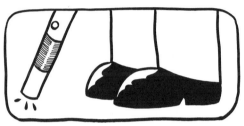

"Yep, that's your blood," said Jeffrey.

Bedbugs live in dark spaces, and are prone to hiding in corners, like in between the pages of books, and any nook and cranny they can fit themselves into.

They emerge from these protective little coffins to feed at night.

They're hard to kill, as they're tough to find, and they aren't very susceptible to poison. They've got to ingest it to die from it, as their exoskeletons keep them protected.

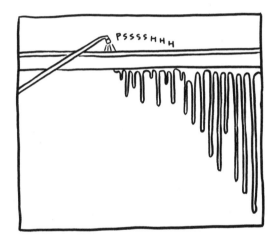

PSSSSHHH

Jeffrey sprayed everything, including the trim above the walls, which proceeded to bleed like something out of a horror movie.

Ilsa came home from wherever she was and grimly threw out everything she owned: clothes, books, furniture.

trash

Cam got the hell out of there and moved into a weekly hotel right around the corner from me.

Throughout all this, I still wasn't sure I had bedbugs.

After all, it's pretty rare for them to travel in clothing. Usually they transport via infested furniture items.

I scoured my apartment for tell-tale signs of The Bug, but found nothing.

No droppings, no molted exoskeletons, no blood on my sheets.

But my bites kept getting worse. Each bite would puff up my whole appendage with painful, itchy redness and swollen glands.

I had almost a dozen bites all over my body!

Friends suggested it might be fleas or mosquitoes, so I closed my windows and checked my kitty for fleas, but the closed windows made the summer heat intolerable, as well as my itching. Oh god, the itching!

Hey, what are you up to?

One night, I found something. A little, soft,
beetle-like bug on my pillow that I instinctively
smooshed.

It smooshed easily, and I came away with a spot
of blood on my hand.

Freaked out, I moved to my couch to sleep, but
just as I was drifting off, I felt something pierce
the skin of my side.

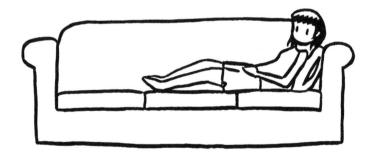

I swatted at whatever it was and came away with
a handful of my own blood.

I called my landlord.

"Please send me an exterminator soon!" I pleaded to his answering machine.

I hadn't slept well in more than a week, plus I was horrified beyond belief.

I'd read about how these bugs work, that they'll feed on a person for **four to seven minutes at a time**. The thought of these creatures piercing my skin for seven-minute stretches triggered my needle-phobia.

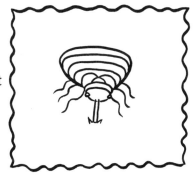

Each time I'd start drifting off to sleep, I'd jolt back awake, full of adrenaline and fear. This would not do.

When the exterminator came, it became clear that this was the same guy, Jeffrey, who'd diagnosed Cam's problem. He didn't seem particularly optimistic about exterminating these bugs.

He found one. Just one.
An adolescent bug, dead in
my closet.

"Teenage suicide," I lamented.
"Don't do it."

I locked my cat in the kitchen
for the next five hours as
Jeffrey sprayed poison all over
my furniture and walls.

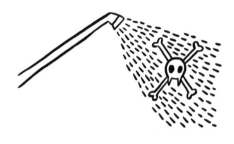

"It'll take a couple of
weeks before they die
off," he said. "If you
don't notice your bites
slowing down by then,
give me a call."

"I should come back in a few weeks anyway to
re-spray for hatchlings, then maybe a few weeks
after that, if they don't go away."

His words gave me no solace.
I kept thinking of the bugs
feeding on me for **four to
seven minutes at a time**, for
months and months and
months. How could I ever
sleep in that apartment again?

216

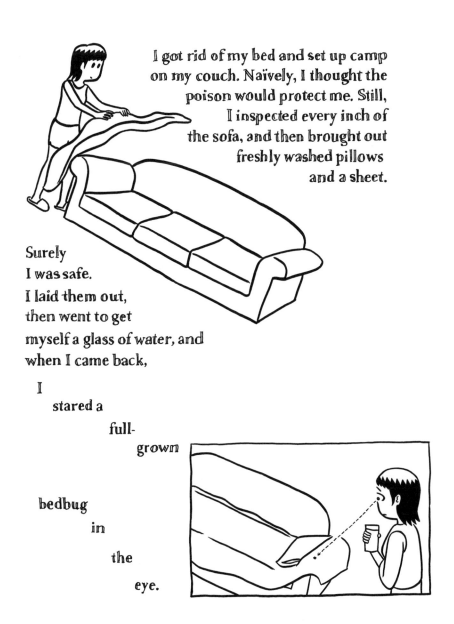

I got rid of my bed and set up camp on my couch. Naïvely, I thought the poison would protect me. Still, I inspected every inch of the sofa, and then brought out freshly washed pillows and a sheet.

Surely
I was safe.
I laid them out,
then went to get
myself a glass of water, and
when I came back,

I
    stared a
            full-
                grown

bedbug
        in
            the
                eye.

217

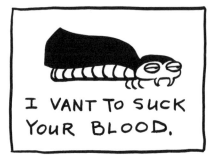

The sonofabitch was waiting for me to fall asleep.

It wanted to eat
me
alive.

For the next few nights I slept in the hotel with Cam, relationship-phobia be damned, with visits during the day to see my cat.

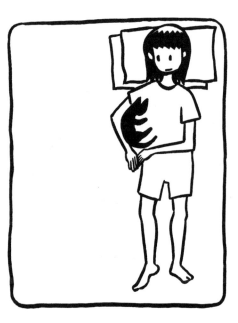

Eventually I graduated to an air mattress, which sucked, but was less painful than the floor and less dangerous than the rapidly accelerating relationship I seemed to be getting myself into.

I gutted my closet, threw out a lot of things, and washed almost all my clothes in hot water. I put the really fancy stuff in plastic bags not to be opened 'til Christmas. Cam helped me go through each LP and sleeve, and many of my books, but we found no bugs.

I don't get it! How am I still getting bitten?

But then over time, the bites began fading away, and then there weren't any new ones.

By this time, I was delirious with lack of sleep and easing into a new love. Despite my earlier reluctance (I was nervous about being a rebound, I was nervous about being another one of Cam's relationship disasters), rabid hormones and Cam's conviction that This Would Work Out had worn me down, and we were now in the thick of it.

But our relationship was very dramatic—highs so high I couldn't see the ground...

...and lows so perplexing and devastating I could barely stand it.

That's when I
noticed that I had
fresh bites
on my arm.

I called the
exterminator
in a panic.

"Hatchlings,"
Jeffrey said
grimly, and he
came back and
re-sprayed,
and said to
call him in a
few weeks if
the bites
started up
again.

I bought a brand-new mattress, but woke up with three new bites the next morning.

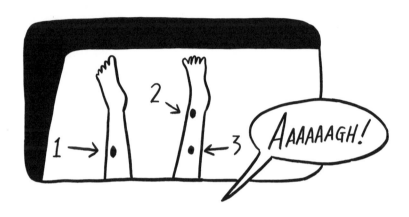

I put double-sided tape at each leg of my bed, and washed everything religiously.

Things got really bad with Cam. He became
emotionally distant and I stopped being rational.

A week later, he broke up with me.

I got rid of every bit of him I could, but some things still lingered.

It took me a year to get rid of the bugs in my home, which is three months longer than I lasted with Cam.

That's a long time to be sleep deprived.

A STRANGER'S HOUSE

KA-CHEE

KA-CHEE!

Let's take a break
while I switch lenses.

Just lift your head up and...

Like this?

Perfect.

KA-CHEE

Now tilt your...

KA-CHEE

So tell me about your...

How long have you been...

Lower your arm just...

...and when I got back, my PTSD was so bad...

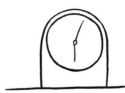

I didn't know where I was.

I just knew they were
            out to
            kill me.

Every morning I woke up
            with my hands
                clenched
                around my
                    wife's neck.

                She'd scream for me
                        to wake up.

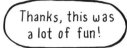

Thanks, this was a lot of fun!

It was my pleasure.

You know...

If you'd like to stick around to review some of these photos, I could give you a ride home after.

Really?

Well, if it's not too much trouble...

Hey.

Are you sure you want to stay here?

I'd like to see those photos!

Okay.

That there's
Richard M. Nixon.

The greatest president
that ever lived.

MARINAOMI 2012

249

COALINGA

IF YOU TAKE HWY. ⑤ FROM LOS ANGELES TO SAN FRANCISCO, YOU WILL PASS BY COALINGA.

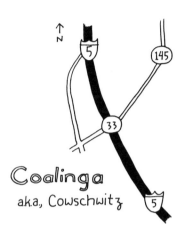

Coalinga
a.k.a, Cowschwitz

THE FIRST THING YOU'LL NOTICE IS THE SMELL.

bug splatter

death
panic
feces
despair

THEN YOU'LL SEE THE COWS.   TENS OF THOUSANDS OF THEM.

WAITING.

BUT THE SMELL...

IT TRIGGERS MY SCENT MEMORY.

IN SEPTEMBER 2005, I WAS RETURNING HOME FROM AN UNPLEASANT VACATION.

THE SMELL GOT WORSE, AND AFTER A COUPLE OF WEEKS,
SOMEONE REALIZED IT WAS COMING FROM THE FIRST FLOOR.

SOFIA'S
APARTMENT.

SOFIA SPENT MOST OF HER TIME IN THE LAUNDRY ROOM...

...SCOWLING.

THEY REMOVED HER BODY, BUT THEY COULDN'T REMOVE THE
MEMORY
OF
HER
SMELL.

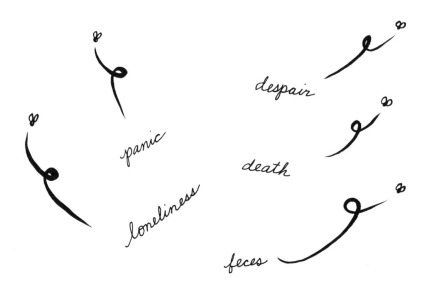

despair

panic

death

loneliness

feces

ONE DAY...

WHOLE

HEARTTHROBS

When I was eleven years old, I traded in my *obsession* for the Beatles for an *obsession* with Duran Duran.

There was so much information available about the band members, I felt as if I knew them all intimately.

One time, my friend and I were walking behind some older girls who went to our middle school.

279

So, Lisa, are you also a painter?

Oh, ha ha! No...

Oh Lisa, my educated, brilliant, SOPHISTICATED friend...

Well, um, I, like, do marketing for, like, an, uh...

ARCHITECTURE firm. Not, um, like, really what I went to school for. Heh.

Earlier today you were determining the futures of multi-million dollar projects...

So then... what subject did you major in at university?

Um, English?

...Tonight you're stumbling over your words like a preteen groupie.

ENGLISH?! Ah ha ha! Every other word that comes out of your mouth is "like"!

Oh the humanity!

Such a strange, sheltered existence a celebrity lives in.

EPILOGUE Much later, at a different party...

Blah blah blah Duran Duran party blah

Oh, I heard about that party.

A friend of mine was there. Apparently it got kind of wild.

Was she the one who stripped off her clothes and jumped into the POOL?

Yeah, that was her!

No shit?!

That's a little gauche, don't you think?

She's not usually like that. She was just having fun. It's not every day you get to party with Duran Duran, right?

I didn't think of it that way...

I should've jumped into the pool too!

©Lisa Thomson 2005

IN CASE OF EMERGENCY

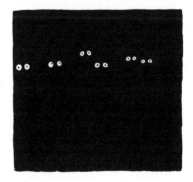

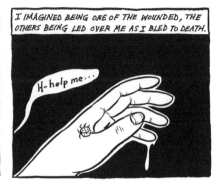

THE SURVIVING PASSENGERS HAD TO STEP OVER BODIES OF THE DEAD AND WOUNDED AS THEY WERE LED TO THE UNDERGROUND TUNNEL.

Groan...

I IMAGINED BEING ONE OF THE WOUNDED, THE OTHERS BEING LED OVER ME AS I BLED TO DEATH.

H-help me...

No, I wouldn't just leave! I would help the wounded!

MY MIND SHIFTED GEARS AND I IMAGINED MYSELF BEING ONE OF THE SURVIVORS.

Help me...

Hmm... What makes a good tourniquet?

↑ ITEMS IN MY LUGGAGE

I IMAGINED FITTING THESE ITEMS GINGERLY OVER HER BLOODY STUMPS AMIDST THE PANIC, THE DARKNESS.

OWWWW!

Hold still.

TIE TIE TIE

THE PROPOSAL

RING SHOPPING

THE JITTERS

THE PROPOSAL

TELLING THE FOLKS

TELLING FRIENDS

HAVE A NICE DAY

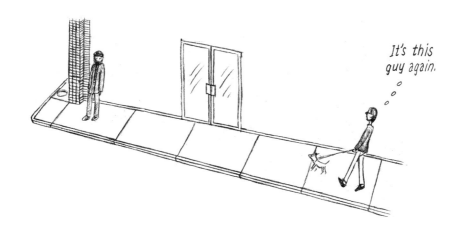

Ugh, but I don't want
to encourage panhandling.

Maybe I should buy
him some FOOD.

Or...

FLASHBACK TO THE EIGHTIES!

Have a
burger.

LATER...

I should've given
him something.

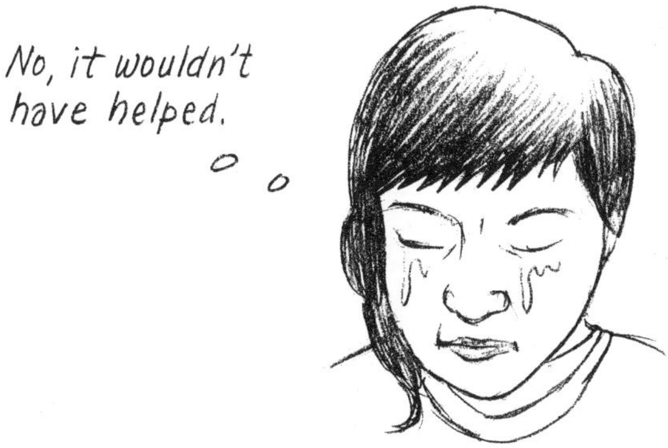
No, it wouldn't have helped.

TWO MONTHS LATER...

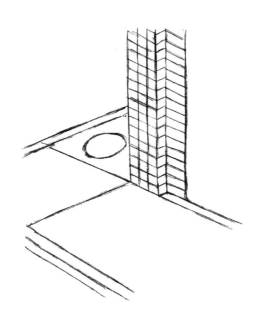

FOR THE GREATER GOOD

Oh man...
Two years ago, this proposi-
tion would've been a no-brainer...

...but now that I'm a homeowner,
voting YES on this feels like
writing a $632.⁰⁰ check to a
school I'll never go to.

And I never even LIKED school!

But I guess formal education is helpful to some people.

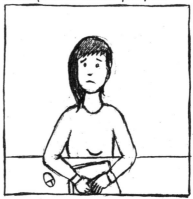

But still...geez!

I'll skip this one and come back to it later.

What the-?!
This measure is ridiculous!

What a surprise...

It was added to the ballot by someone who stands to profit from it. What a jerk.

How can people be so
self-centered?

How can... um...

Ugh.

matw 2012

THE EVIL

Ramada Plaza Inn, April 2012, 3 am

347

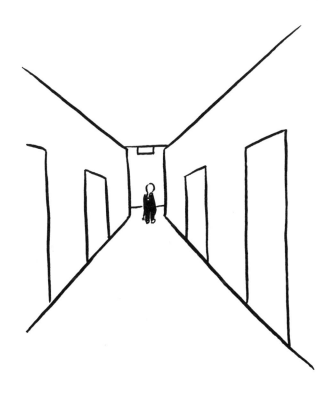

SOBBING

SOBBING

MARINAOMI 2012

367

HAPPY PLACE

WE MOVED TO THIS NEIGHBORHOOD
THREE YEARS AGO.

BUT THEN THIS HAPPENED:

Saturday, January 12, 2013, 7:45 P.M.

A 23-y.o. woman was followed into her
Telegraph Hill home by a man.

He robbed her.

He threatened to kill her.

He did horrible sexual things to her.

Her mother heard
      the whole thing
         on the
           other end of the phone
             and called the cops.

When the police arrived, the woman yelled
to get their attention and the rapist jumped
off her balcony and fled.

A CHP helicopter found him in a neighbor's
backyard using thermal imaging technology
and a spotlight.

He was clutching her backpack, which he had
stolen along with an entire community's
state of well-being.

THE RAPIST IS 25 YEARS OLD.

THE RAPIST IS FROM MARIN CITY.

TWENTY-FIVE YEARS AGO, I SPENT SOME
TIME IN MARIN CITY WITH MY HIGH SCHOOL
BOYFRIEND.

WE SET UP A TENT IN HIS
MOM'S BACKYARD WHERE WE
TICKLED EACH OTHER AND
FOOLED AROUND AND
SHARED OUR DREAMS.

I'D HEARD THERE WAS A LOT OF CRIME IN MARIN CITY.

I HAVE THIS MEMORY OF THE
FIRST TIME I FELT SAFE THERE.

FOR ALL I KNOW, THE RAPIST
MIGHT HAVE BEEN BORN AT
RIGHT THAT VERY MOMENT.

HIS MOM WAS LIKELY HOLDING
HIM IN HER ARMS, LOOKING INTO
HIS PRETTY BROWN EYES.

It doesn't seem
so bad here.

MAYBE SHE WAS WONDERING WHO
HE'D GROW UP TO BE.

MARINAOMI 2013

Acknowledgements

Thanks to the readers and editors of theRumpus.net, where many of these stories originally appeared. Special thanks to Stephen Elliott, Isaac Fitzgerald, Paul Madonna, and Zoë Ruiz, with super-mega-fangirl appreciation for Cheryl Strayed who, as "Dear Sugar," inspired me to dig deep and find the right stories to share.

Big love to Raighne Hogan and Justin Skarhus of 2D Cloud, and my lovely agent, Gordon Warnock of Foreword Literary.

You are the bees' knees.